# Little Book of Patchwork

# LOG CABIN

*Chris Franses*

David & Charles

*Left: Triangle Log Cabin blocks, set to form a Christmas-tree quilt.*

*Opposite: Barn Raising design, made by Liane Purnell.*

A DAVID & CHARLES BOOK

First published in the UK in 2001

Text and designs
Copyright © Christine Franses 2001
Photography and layout
Copyright © David & Charles 2001

A catalogue record for this book is available from the British Library.

ISBN 0 7153 1084 4

Commissioning editor    Cheryl Brown
Text editor             Lin Clements
Book design             Ian Muggeridge
Photography             Stewart Batley

Printed in China by Leefung-Asco Printers Ltd.
for David & Charles
Brunel House  Newton Abbot  Devon

# CONTENTS

## THE BLOCKS

# INTRODUCTION

This book features Log Cabin, one of the most familiar and popular of all patchwork blocks. Simple to make and suitable for all skill levels, it is the infinite number of design possibilities which makes it so exciting to use. From a full-size quilt to a small cushion, with a contemporary or traditional look, there is bound to be a Log Cabin pattern to suit your needs.

## How to Use This Book

The book is one of a series and is intended to fit into your pocket or bag to accompany you on fabric-buying expeditions, rather than be a comprehensive guide to all that is possible. Whilst not providing quilt patterns *per se*, the book features foundation piecing patterns for fifteen blocks. Each of these blocks is illustrated with a 4in block outline, nine possible colourways and eight quilt settings, to encourage you to design your own colour scheme and quilt. There is also a further selection of ten variations on these blocks. A bibliography is provided to point you in the direction of other useful books on the subject of patchwork and quilting, as well as to further patterns.

Clear instructions are given for piecing each individual block and descriptions of a variety of different piecing methods are included. There are details on quilt construction, making sashings, borders and bindings, plus a summary of quilting techniques. Instructions are also included to enable you to draft your own patterns and templates from the ones provided.

Yardage information (in both imperial and metric) is given, with examples, to enable you to calculate how much fabric you need to buy for a project. A minimum purchase of a fat quarter ($\frac{1}{2}$yd/0.5m of fabric cut in half to make two squares) is assumed and seam allowances are taken to be $\frac{1}{4}$in (rounded up to 1cm). The imperial and metric measurements given are not direct equivalents, only approximations, so decide which set of measurements you will use throughout your project.

*Opposite: An off-centre Barn Raising design, made by Liane Purnell.*

# LOG CABIN PATTERNS

Like most patterns, the origins of the Log Cabin are lost in the mists of time. The traditional Log Cabin has a red or yellow centre surrounded by light and dark logs. In the United States the red centre is said to represent the hearth at the centre of the house, the yellow the lamplight, and the light and dark shading the sunshine and shadow on the walls. In Scotland and the Isle of Man the logs are believed to represent the pattern of furrows in the communal medieval fields – the light and dark being the variations in crop growth between the dry and damp ends of the fields.

The traditional Courthouse Steps variation has logs on opposite sides of the block, rather than following round. The centre of this block is often black – for the judge's robes, perhaps. The other traditional variation is the Pineapple block which gives the appearance of being pieced from triangles. The pineapple is a traditional symbol of welcome to a house.

The Log Cabin block has become a firm favourite over the years on both sides of the Atlantic owing to its versatility and the ease with which it can be drawn and sewn. It was, and still is, often constructed on a foundation, enabling a mixture of fabrics to be used; if the foundation were an old blanket then no wadding would be required and the quilt would be made in a 'quilt as you go' method.

At one time logs were often pieced because the quilt was made from precious scraps of fabric; today this technique is deliberately used to create a variety of patterns.

*Opposite: A selection of antique quilts from the collection of Patricia Cox.*

# HOW MUCH FABRIC?

To work out how much fabric you need for a project you need to make several decisions first and then do a few sums. I hope the tables in this section will take some of the complications out of the maths. The yardages given here tend to err on the generous side; once experienced in working out yardages you will be able to buy a little less than is suggested here. A fat quarter, by the way, is a ½yd (0.5m) cut in two to give two 'squares' about 22 × 18in (56 × 50cm). The calculations which follow assume ¼in seams for imperial and 1cm seams for metric measurements. (Please note that imperial and metric measurements in this section are not direct conversions, only equivalents.)

A word of caution before you slice your new fabric into millions of pieces: it really is advisable to make a sample block first, to ensure that the colours you have chosen work together. Sometimes they look great on paper, but in fabric something gets lost, especially using a patterned fabric. Play around until you find a combination that *does* work.

Before you head for the shops however, there are a few questions you need to ask:

**What overall size is your project to be?**
From this you can decide on the size of the block and calculate the number of blocks required. On page 10 are average mattress sizes and the added extra to hang over the edge of the beds to make a suitably sized quilt. If the finished size of the quilt is crucial, measure your mattress to make sure, then add a suitable extra measurement to hang down the sides and foot, and to tuck under the pillow. *See Table page 10*

**What size is the individual block to be?**
First, look at the size of quilt you are making. To use 12in (30cm) blocks in a cot quilt may be tempting but they might be out of proportion; likewise 4in (10cm) blocks in a king size quilt would not be sensible, so choose an individual block size that suits the project.

**How many blocks are needed?**
The number of blocks needed is calculated by multiplying the number of blocks across by the number of blocks down. These figures are

*Opposite: Hidden Star quilt with bold central motifs.*

worked out by dividing the quilt measurements by the block size, shown as follows.

*Example:*

A cot quilt needs:
72 (6 × 9) 4in (10cm) blocks or
24 (4 × 6) 6in (15cm) blocks.
A shorter cot quilt needs:
12 (3 × 4) 8in (20cm) blocks.
A longer cot quilt needs:
15 (3 × 5) 8in (20cm) blocks.
A double quilt needs:
80 (8 × 10) 10in (25cm) blocks or
72 (8 × 9) 10in (25cm) blocks or
56 (7 × 8) 12in (30cm) blocks.

### Are you using sashing between blocks?

If you are using sashing then you will need fewer blocks. One easy way to work this out is to draw the design including the sashing to scale on graph paper, then count up the number of blocks and measure the total width of the sashing.

### How many pieces of each colour and shape are in each block?

You will need to work out the number of pieces of each colour and shape in each block and multiply this by the number of blocks in the quilt to arrive at the *total* number of each colour. This sounds more complicated than it is; with practise you will be able to 'guesstimate' quite accurately the amount of fabric you require.

### How much fabric do I need to buy?

Fabric used for patchwork is generally 44in (112cm) wide but check this, because if it is less you will probably need to buy more than I have indicated in the examples that follow. Work out the number of logs of each length (including the seam allowance) you can cut from one width of fabric. Divide the number of these logs you need by the number of logs cut from one strip and you know how many strips to cut. Knowing the width of the strips

|  | *Mattress size* | *Quilt size* |
|---|---|---|
| Cot | 22 × 45in (55 × 115cm) | 24 × 36in (60 × 90cm) |
| Single (twin) | 36 × 72in (90 × 180cm) | 60 × 92in (150 × 235cm) |
| Double | 54 × 72in (135 × 180cm) | 80 × 96in (205 × 245cm) |
| King | 60 × 78in (150 × 200cm) | 102 × 102in (260 × 260cm) |

## Table 1 – Logs from a 44in (112cm) wide strip

| Cut length | Finished length | Number of logs |
| --- | --- | --- |
| 1½in (4.5cm) | 1in (2.5cm) | 29 (24) |
| 2in (6cm) | 1½in (4cm) | 22 (18) |
| 2½in (7cm) | 2in (5cm) | 17 (16) |
| 3in (8cm) | 2½in (6cm) | 14 (14) |
| 3½in (9.5cm) | 3in (7.5cm) | 12 (11) |
| 4in (11cm) | 3½in (9cm) | 11 (10) |
| 4½in (12cm) | 4in (10cm) | 9 (9) |
| 5in (13.5cm) | 4½in (11.5cm) | 8 (8) |
| 5½in (14.5cm) | 5in (12.5cm) | 8 (7) |
| 6in (16cm) | 5½in (14cm) | 7 (7) |
| 6½in (17cm) | 6in (15cm) | 6 (6) |
| 7in (18.5cm) | 6½in (16.5cm) | 6 (6) |
| 7½in (20cm) | 7in (18cm) | 5 (5) |
| 8in (21cm) | 7½in (19cm) | 5 (5) |
| 8½in (22cm) | 8in (20cm) | 5 (5) |
| 9in (23.5cm) | 8½in (21.5cm) | 4 (4) |
| 9½in (25cm) | 9in (23cm) | 4 (4) |
| 10in (26cm) | 9½in (24cm) | 4 (4) |
| 10½in (27.5cm) | 10in (25.5cm) | 4 (4) |
| 11in (29cm) | 10½in (27cm) | 4 (3) |
| 11½in (30cm) | 11in (28cm) | 3 (3) |
| 12in (31cm) | 11½in (29cm) | 3 (3) |
| 12½in (32cm) | 12in (30cm) | 3 (3) |

you are cutting means you can work out how much fabric to buy.

*Example:*

If you need to cut fifteen 10in (25cm) long by 4in (10cm) wide logs (including seam allowances), then you can cut four logs from one 44in (112cm) wide piece of fabric. You therefore need to cut four strips to give you sixteen logs. Multiply the number of strips by their width – four × 4in (four × 10cm) – to give the amount of fabric to buy = 16in (40cm). Adding a bit for mistakes and to

allow for the shop to cut the fabric off the grain means you should buy ½yd (0.5m).

**How many logs can I cut from one strip of 44in (112cm) wide fabric?**
(Note that the cut lengths quoted below include seam allowances.) *See Table 1 page 11*

**How many squares can be cut from specific lengths of fabric?**
You need to be able to calculate the number of squares that can be cut from a fat quarter,

**TABLE 2 – Squares**

| Cut size | Finished size | Fat quarter Number | ½yd (0.5m) Number | ¾yd (0.75m) Number | 1yd (1m) Number |
|---|---|---|---|---|---|
| 1½in (4.5cm) | 1in (2.5cm) | 168 (132) | 348 (264) | 522 (384) | 696 (528) |
| 2½in (7cm) | 2in (5cm) | 56 (56) | 119 (112) | 170 (160) | 238 (224) |
| 3½in (9.5cm) | 3in (7.5cm) | 30 (25) | 60 (55) | 84 (77) | 120 (110) |
| 4½in (12cm) | 4in (10cm) | 16 (16) | 36 (36) | 54 (54) | 72 (72) |

**TABLE 3 – Folded triangles**

| Cut size | Finished size | Fat quarter Number | ½yd (0.5m) Number | ¾yd (0.75m) Number | 1yd (1m) Number |
|---|---|---|---|---|---|
| 2in (6cm) | 1½in (4cm) | 99 (72) | 198 (144) | 286 (216) | 396 (288) |
| 3in (8cm) | 2½in (6cm) | 42 (42) | 84 (84) | 126 (126) | 168 (168) |
| 4in (11cm) | 3½in (9cm) | 20 (20) | 44 (40) | 66 (60) | 99 (90) |

from ½yd (0.5m), from ¾yd (0.75m) and from 1yd (1m). These squares will be needed as the central squares in a Log Cabin block or for Stepping Stones. *See Table 2*

### How many squares can be cut from specific lengths of fabric to make folded triangles?

You will need to cut squares to make folded triangles for Marching Triangles, Log Cabin Ribbons and Wild Goose. Table 3 gives you the number produced from the various lengths of fabric. *See Table 3*

### How many right-angled triangles (half-squares) can be cut from specific lengths of fabric?

You will need to cut right-angled triangles (half-square) for Marching Triangles, Log Cabin Ribbons, Wild Goose, Split-centre Log Cabin, Pineapple etc. Table 4 gives you the number produced from the various lengths of fabric. Note, the numbers yielded in metric are more or less the same as the imperial. *See Table 4*

### TABLE 4 – Right-angled triangles

| Cut size | Finished size | Fat Quarter Number | ½yd (0.5m) Number | ¾yd (0.75m) Number | 1yd (1m) Number |
|---|---|---|---|---|---|
| 1⅞in (6cm) | 1in (2.5cm) | 108 | 396 | 572 | 792 |
| 2⅜in (7.5cm) | 1½in (4cm) | 98 | 238 | 340 | 476 |
| 2⅞in (8.5cm) | 2in (5cm) | 72 | 168 | 252 | 336 |
| 3⅜in (9.5cm) | 2½in (6cm) | 50 | 120 | 168 | 240 |
| 3⅞in (11cm) | 3in (7.5cm) | 32 | 88 | 132 | 198 |
| 4⅜in (12.5cm) | 3½in (9cm) | 32 | 72 | 108 | 144 |
| 4⅞in (13.5cm) | 4in (10cm) | 18 | 48 | 80 | 112 |
| 5⅜in (15cm) | 4½in (11.5cm) | 18 | 48 | 64 | 96 |
| 5⅞in (16cm) | 5in (12.5cm) | 18 | 42 | 56 | 84 |

# Worked Example 1 – Cot Quilt
(Imperial measurements)

**Overall Size:** 30in square approximately. This size will allow for a good tuck in at the sides, but not be so long that the baby can pull it over its face.

**Quilt Pattern:** Traditional log cabin block, straight set, no sashing or borders, in rainbow colours.

**Block Size:** If I use 8in blocks then I can make a quilt 32in square, using 4 blocks across by 4 blocks down (4 × 8in = 32), i.e. 16 blocks total.

**Calculations:** From my drawing *(see plan opposite)* I can see that I need 16 of each colour log and central square. The square is cut 2½in and the logs are cut 1½in wide. Measuring the length of each log I find they are cut 2½in, 3½in, 4½in, 5½in, 6½in, 7½in and 8½in long. Looking at Table 1 on page 11, I can see the number of each log I can cut from a width of fabric and therefore I can work out how much of each fabric I need to buy.

• I can cut 56 2½in squares from a fat quarter of fabric; therefore one fat quarter will be ample for my central squares (see Table 2 page 12).

• I can cut 29 1½in logs from one strip of 44in wide fabric, or 14 from one strip of a fat quarter (22in × 18in); therefore one fat quarter of yellow fabric will be ample (see Table 1).

• I can cut 5 8½in logs from one width of 44in wide fabric, so I will need to cut four strips to get 16 logs (4 × 1½ = 6in), therefore a ¼yd is ample for this longest piece (the dark green). I can cut two logs from one fat quarter strip. I need to cut eight strips to get 16 logs (8 × 1½ = 12). A fat quarter is (usually) 18in, therefore a fat quarter is enough for the dark green logs as well.

• My fabric shopping list indicates that I can cut this cot quilt out from a collection of fat quarters; plus 1yd/m of backing fabric and 1yd/m of wadding (batting).

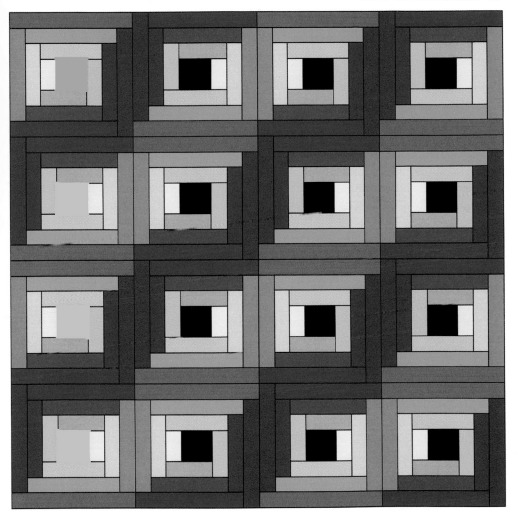

# Worked Example 2 – Christmas Wall Hanging
### (Metric measurements)

**Overall Size:** 80 × 80cm

**Quilt Pattern:** Hidden Star Log Cabin

**Block Size:** If I use 20cm blocks I need 16 blocks altogether for my design. The logs are 2.5cm wide and the central square is 5cm. I am using three different reds, three different greens and one white print.

**Calculations:** First, I work out how many of each colour piece I need. I will need to cut 16 central white squares, 36 smaller white squares and 72 white triangles for the stars *(see plan opposite)*.

• From Table 2, I see I can cut 56 central squares (7cm cut size) from one fat quarter of fabric (56 × 50cm).

• From Table 2, I can cut 132 smaller squares (4.5cm cut size) from a fat quarter and from Table 4 page 13, 108 triangles (6cm cut size). I can cut both of these from one fat quarter.

• I need to cut 16 of each size and colour of log. From my first red, I need to cut logs to finish at 5cm and at 7.5cm. Looking at Table 1 on page 11, I can cut all these from 13.5cm of fabric or from a fat quarter.

• From my first green, I need to cut logs to finish at 7.5cm and 10cm. I can cut these from a fat quarter too.

• From the second red, I need logs to finish at 10cm and 12.5cm. These can be cut from 22.5cm of fabric or at a pinch from a fat quarter. I think I would ask for a 25cm.

• From the second green, I need to cut logs to finish at 12.5cm and 15cm. According to Table 1, I will need 27cm for this – slightly more than 25cm.

• For the third red, I will need to cut logs to finish at 15cm and, for the outside edges, 17.5cm and 20cm. From Table 1, I calculate that I will need about 45cm. I also need to bind the quilt and this will use up another four strips 7cm wide (45 + 28 = 73cm). I could get away with 75cm, but for safety will buy 1m.

• For the last green I need to cut 32 logs to finish at 15cm. From Table 1, I see I will need to buy 27cm.

• So my fabric shopping list will read:

Central squares = 1 fat quarter (white or something else perhaps).

Stars = 1 fat quarter (white).

Red logs and binding = 1 fat quarter, 25cm and 1m.

Green logs = 1 fat quarter, 30cm, and 30cm.

Backing and wadding (batting) = 1m each.

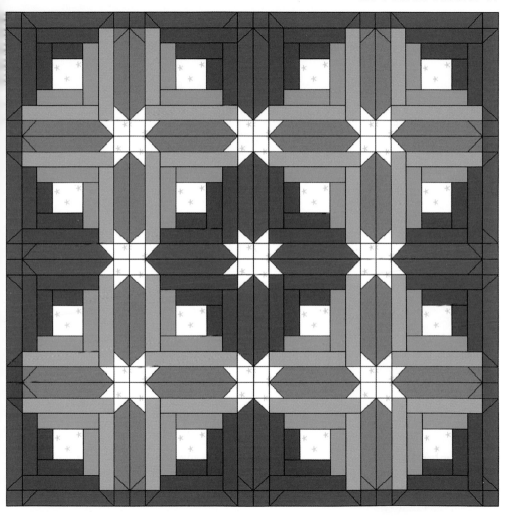

# TECHNIQUES

This section contains information on the basic patchworking techniques you will need to master in order to make a Log Cabin quilt. Where necessary for clarity, figures are marked WS (wrong side) and RS (right side).

## USING THE BLOCK TEMPLATES

Log Cabin blocks, on the whole, are made from strips of fabric with a central square, although occasionally triangles or other squares are added to create secondary patterns. The strips are generally all the same width, although some variations use different width strips, e.g. Off-Centre Log Cabin.

The fifteen blocks described in this book are accompanied by 4in block outlines. You can use the outline pattern directly as a foundation piecing pattern – just trace or photocopy it onto your foundation (see Making Templates below). Further Variations, beginning on page 122, illustrates yet more patterns and colourways for you to experiment with.

If you want larger blocks or a metric block, the patterns are very easy to draw using the appropriate graph paper. Follow the proportions for the blocks – for example the central square in traditional Log Cabin is usually twice the width of the strips – and use the graph paper as a guideline to draw accurate-sized templates for each block. For ordinary machine or speed machine piecing, the only templates you will need will be the measurement for the central squares, the width of the strips for rotary cutting, and any other shapes – such as the triangles in Wild Goose. Of course, you can always enlarge the drawings given on a photocopier, but be aware that photocopying can distort very slightly, so check the block to make sure before sewing.

Another way to make the block larger is to simply add more rounds of logs until the block reaches the required size.

## MAKING TEMPLATES

The cheapest material for making templates is card, such as that from cereal boxes. Trace your pattern pieces onto tracing paper, glue this onto card and carefully cut out the shape. You can also mark the grain lines on templates where appropriate. The main drawback of card templates is that the more you draw round them, the more you wear them away, which will alter the shape and size gradually – something you may not notice until you try to join the first piece you cut out to the last one. Special transparent template plastic can be bought from quilting suppliers and is an ideal, long-lasting solution. It is placed over the patterns to be traced and the shapes drawn with pencil before cutting out. It is also useful for cutting out from motif fabric as you can see exactly where the motif will finish up.

Remember always to label your templates. Another good idea is to keep the templates for a particular block, or set of blocks, in a small plastic bag, together with the instructions for making the block.

## CUTTING THE FABRIC

The easiest and quickest way to cut fabric strips is to use a rotary cutter, although it is perfectly possible to use a ruler, pencil and scissors to mark and cut (or tear) the strips.

As with most things it takes practise to be able to use a rotary cutter efficiently and effectively. Stock up with some old sheets, or fabric you hate, and practise cutting these first before attempting to rotary cut your masterpiece. Many books on rotary cutting are available, but the main points to remember are to ensure that the fabric is straight before cutting strips, otherwise the strips will have kinks in, and to use the cutter firmly and confidently, cutting from one edge of the fabric to the other against the ruler, ensuring that you cut through all the layers.

## PIECING THE BLOCKS

This can be done by hand or machine. The construction of the Log Cabin block is fairly straightforward and lends itself very readily to machine piecing. It is an excellent way to familiarise yourself with machining straight seams and enjoy yourself at the same time. Take care with the seam allowances as the slightest variation when multiplied up across the block can make quite a difference to the finished block size.

Having cut your strips and central squares, lay them out carefully in the correct sequence

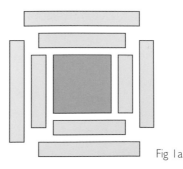

Fig 1a

for sewing (Fig 1a), perhaps pinning them to a cork or polystyrene tile. For hand piecing you may prefer to cut each strip to the required length, but for quick machine piecing leave the strips as they were cut. Keep a coloured diagram of your project to hand so you can check quickly whether you are sewing the right pieces each time and decide whether the pattern is to be sewn clockwise or anticlockwise. The direction doesn't matter as long as you are consistent. It will probably depend on whether you are right- or left-handed.

If the pattern you have chosen has pieced logs – for example the log has squares added to the ends or is composed of two smaller rectangles – then piece the logs first before constructing the block (see speed piecing triangles on logs, page 22).

**Hand Piecing**

Take the central square and put the first log in place on top, right sides together (Fig 1b). You may like to pin the seam. Start with a knot or a couple of backstitches at the end of the seam and sew a small neat running stitch with an occasional backstitch (the piecing stitch) to the end of the seam line. Finish with a small knot or a couple of backstitches to secure the thread. Finger press the seam to one side – to the darker fabric if possible. Continue to add logs in the same fashion, following the pattern round in the same direction (Fig 1c). When the last log is stitched in place, press the seams carefully.

**Machine Piecing**

Take the central square and put the first log in place on top, right sides together. Stitch along the seam, using a medium-length stitch from one raw edge to the end. Don't make the stitches too small or you will be unable to unpick any mistakes; too long and they will come undone easily. There is no need to mark seam allowances for machine piecing, just use the seam guide markings on the sewing machine or use a piece of masking tape as a guide. There is no need to fasten off the threads – as you sew over each seam end this will secure it. Finger press or iron the seam to

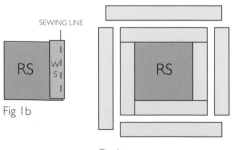

SEWING LINE

RS

WS

Fig 1b

RS

Fig 1c

one side – to the darker fabric if possible. Continue to add the logs, in sequence, in the same way until the block is complete. Press the seams carefully.

**Speed Piecing**

This is useful when piecing a large number of identical blocks. Cut out the central squares but don't cut the strips into individual logs. Take the strip for the first log and lay the first central square on top, right sides together and lining up the raw edges. Stitch in place and put the next square down on the strip without removing the strip from the machine, cutting the threads, or even lifting the needle (Fig 2a). Continue to sew down the length of the strip adding each square in turn until all the squares have been sewn to the strip. If you are making a lot of blocks you may need to cut two strips.

Press the seam to one side all down the length of the strip (Fig 2b) and take the strip with all the squares attached to the cutting board. Use the rotary cutter and ruler to slice the squares apart, together with the first log (Fig 2c).

Now, take the second log strip and place it right side up on the machine. Using one of the pieces cut at stage 2c, put this on top (turned sideways), right sides down and

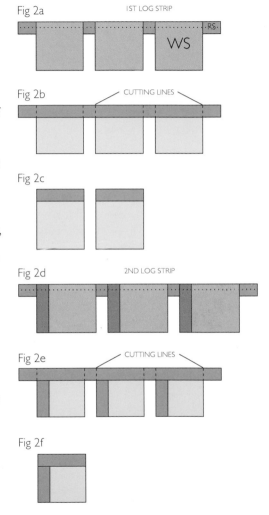

Fig 2a — 1ST LOG STRIP — RS. — WS

Fig 2b — CUTTING LINES

Fig 2c

Fig 2d — 2ND LOG STRIP

Fig 2e — CUTTING LINES

Fig 2f

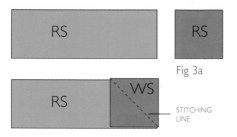

Fig 3a

STITCHING LINE

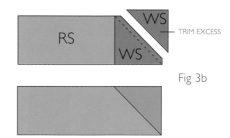

TRIM EXCESS

Fig 3b

stitch in place (Fig 2d). Continue adding the squares as before until all the squares are sewn to the second log. Take care that you are sewing the log to the correct side of the squares each time. Slice the squares apart as before (Fig 2e and 2f). Continue adding the logs in the same way until the blocks are complete.

**Speed Piecing Triangles on the Ends of the Log**

Cut a square to the finished size of the triangle plus the seam allowance, i.e. for a 3in triangle cut a 3½in square. Place this on top of the log, right sides together, at the end, and stitch across the diagonal (Fig 3a). Trim the excess zowance (Fig 3b), then press the triangle back to complete.

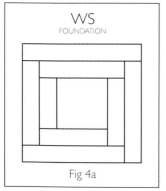

Fig 4a

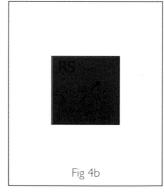

Fig 4b

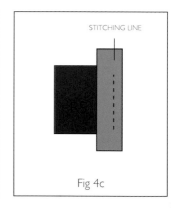

Fig 4c

## Foundation Piecing

This means piecing the block on a foundation – usually of paper, lightweight Vilene or fine cotton. A foundation of warm sheeting or an old blanket could also be used in a 'quilt-as-you-go' fashion. The advantage of foundation piecing is the accuracy obtained, plus it provides a stable base to enable the use of such diverse fabrics as silk and velvet in the same piece. Foundation-piecing Vilene can be bought from specialist shops, as can rubber stamps to facilitate accurate marking.

Begin by marking the pattern on the foundation (Fig 4a), bearing in mind that the block will be a mirror image of the marked block and that, unless the foundation is paper, it will not be removed, so chose a suitable fabric marker i.e. not a biro.

Take the first fabric – the central square – and place it, right side up, on the plain, unmarked side of the foundation, so that it covers the central square marking (Fig 4b). Pin it in place. Take the fabric for the first log, trim it roughly to size and place right side down on top of the central square, so that when it is stitched and flipped right sides up it covers the marked area (Fig 4c). Stitch along the seam line on the marked side of the foundation (Fig 4d). Turn the foundation over to the fabric side, flip the first log back into position, press the seam, and trim the piece if necessary (Fig 4e).

Take the second log fabric and cut it roughly to the size of the second log. Place it right side down along the correct seam line on the plain side of the foundation, so that

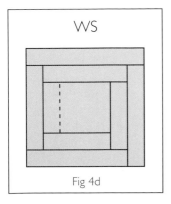

Fig 4d

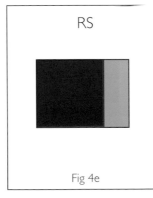

Fig 4e

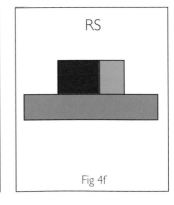

Fig 4f

when it is stitched it can be flipped back in place and will cover the marked area (Fig 4f). Stitch along the seam line marked on the foundation (Fig 4g). Turn the foundation over to the fabric, flip the second log back, press the seam and trim the piece to size if necessary (Fig 4h). Continue this way until the block is complete.

**Quilt as You Go**

This method is foundation piecing taken a stage further. You could use an old blanket or flannelette sheeting for the foundation or a piece of wadding (batting) with a marked backing. You can use the backingas the actual backing for the quilt or you can add a separate backing after the quilt is finished,

however, this will not show the quilting and will only be attached to the quilt around the edges.

Mark the block on a foundation or the quilt block backing and pin or tack (baste) the wadding on top. Proceed as for foundation piecing, but place the fabric pieces on top of the wadding. As you stitch each log in place you will also quilt it!

**Folded Log Cabin**

There are two methods of constructing a Log Cabin block using folded fabric for the logs. Method 1 gives a flatter effect while Method 2 is more textured. To reduce the bulk in the final seams (for joining blocks together) use ordinary unfolded logs for the final round.

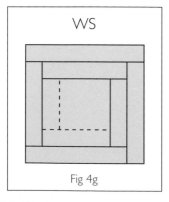

Fig 4g

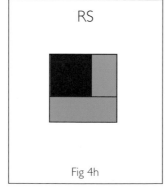

Fig 4h

## Folded Log Cabin *Method 1*

*Method 2*

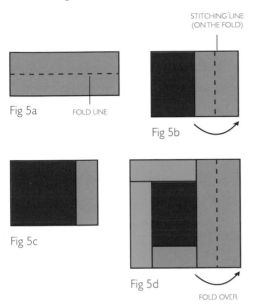

STITCHING LINE
(ON THE FOLD)

Fig 5a  FOLD LINE

Fig 5b

Fig 5c

Fig 5d  FOLD OVER

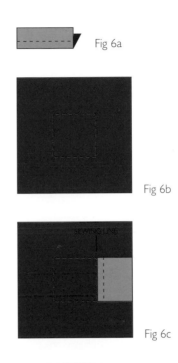

Fig 6a

Fig 6b

SEWING LINE

Fig 6c

*Method 1* You will need to cut the logs twice their finished width plus your seam allowance – for example a 1in log with a ¼in seam allowance should be cut 2½in. (A 2.5cm log with a 1cm seam allowance should be cut 7cm.)

Fold all the logs in half lengthways, press and open them out again (Fig 5a). Place the first log so that the centre fold lies along the stitching line on the central square (Fig 5b). Stitch into place and then fold the log back

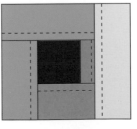

Fig 6d

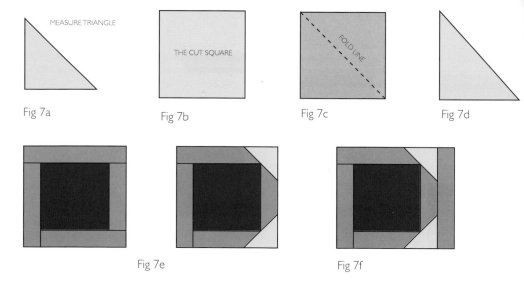

Fig 7a

Fig 7b

Fig 7c

Fig 7d

Fig 7e

Fig 7f

(Fig 5c). Repeat for all the first round logs.

Place the first log of the next round so that the centre fold line lies along the stitching line (Fig 5d). Stitch and fold back. Continue in this fashion until the block is complete.

*Method 2* This works best with narrow logs – about ½in (1.25cm) of log showing. Cut all the logs twice their finished width plus a ¾in (2cm) seam allowance. So, for a ½in (1.25cm) log this would be 2½in (6.5cm), that is ½in × 2, plus ¾in × 2 (or in metric, 1.25cm × 2, plus 2cm × 2). Cut the central square

with a ¾in (2cm) seam allowance as well.

Fold all the logs in half lengthways and press (Fig 6a). Mark a sewing line on the central square and on the logs ¾in (2cm) from the raw edges (Fig 6b). Now place the first log so that the fold lies along the marked line on the central square and stitch along the marked stitching line on the log (Fig 6c). Place the second log so that the fold is on the marked line on the central square and stitch in place along the line marked on the log. Sew the remaining two logs in place in the same way.

For the next round, place the first log so that the fold lies along the stitching line of the previous round. Stitch along the marked seam line on the log (Fig 6d). Continue in this fashion until the block is complete.

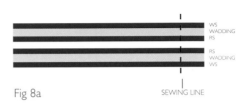

Fig 8a

### Folded Triangles

Used in blocks such as Wild Goose, these are easy to make. Measure the finished size of the triangle you need (Fig 7a) and cut a square to this measurement plus a seam allowance (Fig 7b). Now fold the square in half along the diagonal (Fig 7c) and the folded triangle is ready to be stitched in place (Fig 7d).

Sew the first round of logs and then place the folded triangle in position (the fold facing the centre), tacking (basting) or pinning it in place (Fig 7e). Sew the next round of logs in place, catching the folded triangles into the seam allowance as you do so (Fig 7f).

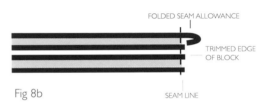

Fig 8b

### JOINING QUILT-AS-YOU-GO BLOCKS

Place the two blocks right sides together and stitch the seam (Fig 8a). Trim the wadding (batting) back to the seam line. Trim the seam allowance on one block back to ¼inch (1cm). Press under the other backing fabric seam allowance by ¼inch (1cm) (Fig 8b). Slip stitch this seam allowance over the adjacent block (Fig 8c).

Fig 8c

SEAM OF TUBE

Fig 9a

SLIP STITCHING

RS          RS

Fig 9b      TUBE OF MATCHING BACKING FABRIC

## Joining Blocks into Quilts

On the whole, Log Cabin quilts do not have sashing strips – strips that separate the blocks – and frequently do not have borders either. Blocks are joined straight together, or occasionally on point, to form a design. Many examples of possible quilt settings are given for each of the fifteen main blocks.

To make a 4 × 4 quilt without sashing, join the blocks together using your chosen seam allowance into pairs at first, then join the pairs into fours. These fours can then be joined to gradually build up the completed quilt.

To make a quilt with rows of three, join the blocks into pairs at first then add the odd ones to each pair to make a row of three. Join the rows into pairs, then into fours before joining the last ones together. Try to avoid sewing a small unit – one block or one row – onto a much larger unit.

### Adding Sashing Strips

Some patterns look better if sashing strips are used to separate the blocks or groups of blocks. Ideally the sashing strips will be the same width as, or narrower than, the logs in the blocks. If using sashing to separate groups of blocks, piece these groups first and then treat as a single unit. Lay the blocks (or units) out in order, then sew a sashing

Alternatively, after stitching the seam, you can trim both seam allowances back to ¼inch (1cm). Make a tube of matching backing fabric from a strip cut 1 inch (2.5cm) wide, press it so that the seam is in the centre underneath (Fig 9a). Place this tube over the join on the back of the blocks and slip stitch it in place to cover the seam (Fig 9b). There are many ways to join these blocks together and most books will give further instructions.

strip to the right-hand side of each block except the one on the end of the row. Now sew the blocks into rows.

Stitch a sashing strip to the bottom of each row except the last and now sew the rows together – into pairs, then fours and so on.

## Adding Borders

If you are adding a border, the width needs to be in proportion to the quilt blocks and to the sashing. You can have just one border, or multiple borders. One narrow border with a wide, outer border can look effective.

To make a simple squared-corner border (as opposed to mitred corners), measure your quilt down the centre and cut two strips this length from your fabric. Pin these border strips carefully to the two side edges of your quilt, matching the centre of the strip with the centre of the quilt edge – this will 'square up' your quilt so that it hangs properly. Using a ¼in (1cm) seam allowance, sew these strips to the two side edges of the quilt, then press the seams to one side.

Now measure across the middle of the quilt and use this measurement to cut strips for the top and bottom. Again pin the strips in place matching the ends and centres and sew using a ¼in (1cm) seam allowance. Press the seams to one side.

## QUILTING

Once the quilt top is pieced, it can be quilted in a number of ways. Fine hand quilting, however, is not really an option for Log Cabin as there are too many seams to make a success of it. Instead, consider machine quilting, tie quilting or big stitch quilting (all described below).

Begin by deciding on a quilting design and, if necessary, marking this on the quilt top in a form that will easily wash out. Log Cabin quilts can be quilted by following the design of the quilt, for example, quilting around the centre squares and around each block or flying goose or star. An alternative is to ignore the quilt top pattern and impose a different quilting design on top. Curves, diagonal lines or a wave pattern can all look effective. You could also quilt motifs at intervals on the quilt – in the central squares perhaps.

### Tacking (Basting)

Cut the quilt wadding (batting) and backing about 1in (2.5cm) larger all round than the quilt top. Press the backing and quilt top then spread the backing out on a large flat surface, right side down. If possible fasten the backing fabric down – with masking tape or pin it to the carpet if you are working on the floor – so that it remains taut and wrinkle free while you tack the layers together. Place the wadding centrally on the backing and the quilt top, right side up, on top of the wadding. Pin with safety pins or tack (baste) the three layers together in a grid pattern to hold them together. Start from the centre and work out to the edges, smoothing out the wrinkles as you go.

### Machine Quilting

It is best to start with a small practice piece first to ensure that your machine is set up correctly, using the same weight backing, wadding (batting) and top fabric as for the quilt. Set the machine up for darning if you are going to do free machining, otherwise, for straight-stitch quilting fit the walking foot (or easy-feed foot) to your machine. You will probably need to loosen the top tension slightly and, on some machines, tighten the bottom tension. This is to ensure that the stitch lies flat in the work and no loops of bottom thread show on the top.

Start with the stitch length set to virtually zero and gradually increase it to a fairly long stitch. Follow the quilting line as accurately as you can and finish by gradually decreasing the stitch length down to zero again. These tiny stitches are almost impossible to pull out

and will be secure enough for a quilt that won't get much wear and tear. For a quilt that will be washed regularly, knot the thread ends and lose them in the wadding as you would for hand quilting.

### Tie Quilting

This form of quilting gives a puffy effect to the quilt by fastening the three layers together at discrete intervals with a knotted thread. Use an embroidery or crochet thread and a large needle – you may find a curved needle is easier. Place the needle where you want the tie to be (at the junction of two logs perhaps) and take one stitch through all three layers, leaving a long tail of thread at the beginning. Take another stitch in the same place, pull it tight, and cut off the thread, leaving a long tail. Tie the two tail threads together using a reef knot if possible, although a granny knot is acceptable. Leave the ends free – you may want to trim them. These free ends can be on top of the quilt or underneath depending on the effect you wish to create. Alternatively, you can thread the ends into the wadding (batting) so that the knot is all but hidden.

To emphasise the ties you could use narrow ribbon tied in bows, or tie big-looped bows using embroidery threads in contrasting colours. Another way to tie the quilt is to use buttons and either sew these at intervals or combine them with big, knotted ties. Buttons are not recommended for quilts to be used by young children.

**Big-stitch Quilting**

As its name implies, this form of hand quilting does not involve doing the smallest stitch you can. Just use a contrasting embroidery or crochet thread and stitch your design over the quilt using a neat running stitch. The stitches should be a sensible size – not toe catchers, but certainly not twelve to the inch – and evenly spaced as they would be for fine hand quilting. You will find that the thickness of the thread, the size of the needle and the thickness of the quilt will dictate the size of stitch you can achieve. With this form of quilting you can create all-over patterns or quilt contrasting motifs over your log cabins. Try quilting circles over a very geometric design for an interesting effect.

**BINDING AND FINISHING**

To finish the quilt, cut two strips of binding fabric 2in (5cm) wide and the length of the two sides of the quilt. Fold them in half lengthways, wrong sides together, and press.

Pin the binding strips to the two sides of the quilt, matching the raw edges and stitch ⅝in (1.5cm) away from the raw edges. Now roll the folded edge to the back of the quilt, pin and slip stitch in place. Make sure the stitches do not go right through to the front of the quilt.

Cut two more 2in (5cm) wide strips, this time about 1in (2.5cm) longer than the top and bottom. Fold in half and press as before. Pin in place along the top and bottom edges allowing 1in (2.5cm) to overlap at each end. Stitch in place ⅝in (1.5cm) from the raw edges. Once again, roll the folded edge over to the back of the quilt to pin and slip stitch in place. As you do so, fold the overlap of the binding to the back of the quilt to make a neat finished corner with no raw edges showing.

Finally, and most importantly, make a label for the back of the quilt, stating who made it and when. You can add other information if you wish.

# TRADITIONAL LOG CABIN

The traditional Log Cabin block consists of a central square (often red in colour) around which is stitched a series of rectangles (the logs) – at least two rounds but three, four or more is more usual.

Traditional Log Cabin blocks can be put together to create a wide variety of patterns, each with their own names. The quilt settings on pages 36–7 show some of them.

This block is usually coloured so that it is split diagonally half-light and half-dark. The same colours in different shades can be used, two contrasting colours, or even a mixture of colours and patterns – a useful way to use up those left over strips from other projects.

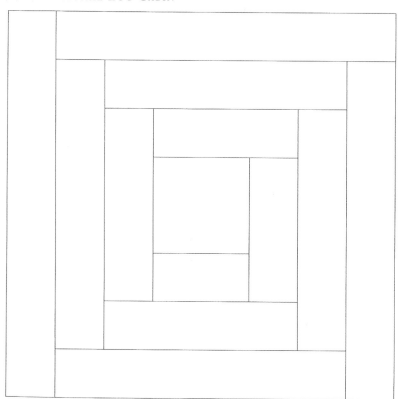

**Colourways**

The colourways, right, show how the centre square colour can make the area recede or advance. The log colours too alter the look, emphasising half the block or creating spirals or squares.

**Quilt Settings**

Running clockwise from top left, the eight quilt settings overleaf (straight set, without sashing), show some of the variations possible – straight furrows, barn raising, sunshine and shadow, star, streak o' lightning, triangles, pinwheel and confrontation or seahorses.

**Block Pattern**

To construct the block use the 4in pattern here as a guide and follow the instructions given in Techniques for your chosen method – hand, machine, foundation piecing or quilt-as-you-go. Start with the central square and sew the first log in place. Then, move clockwise around, sewing the logs in turn to complete the block.

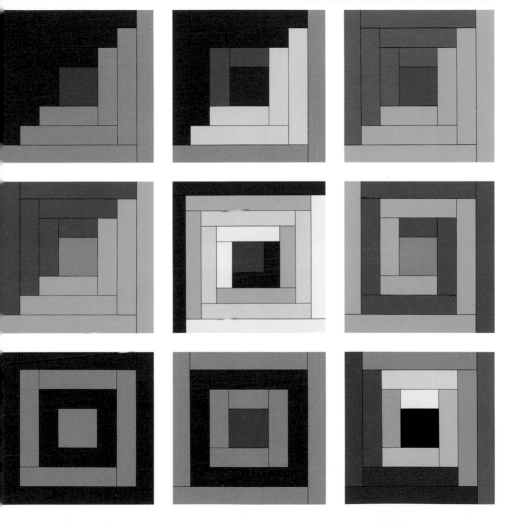

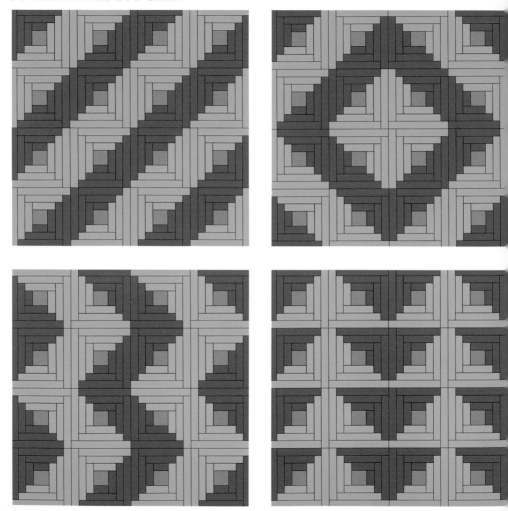

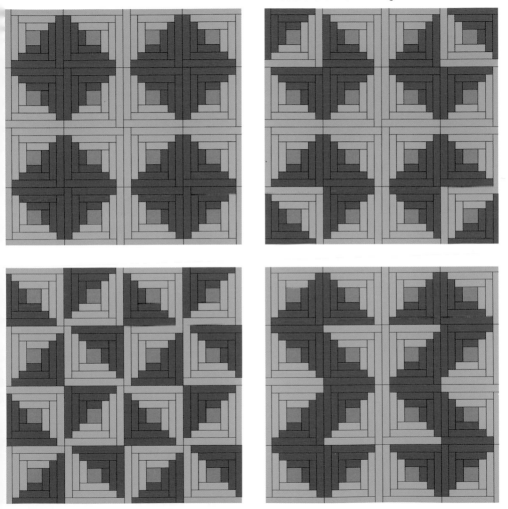

# COURTHOUSE STEPS

Traditionally, the centre of this block is black to indicate the judge's robes, the focus of the design. Arranged around this square, the logs or 'steps' are usually of just two contrasting colours, to emphasise and lead up to the solemn courthouse. This simple approach is illustrated in the first two colourways shown overleaf. By varying the colours, the look of the block can be altered in a number of interesting ways, as shown in the quilt settings on pages 42–3.

This method of adding strips to the central square – alternately, rather than in sequence – can be used to create other Log Cabin-type designs around shapes other than a square. Try this method around a rectangle, hexagon, or octagon for instance.

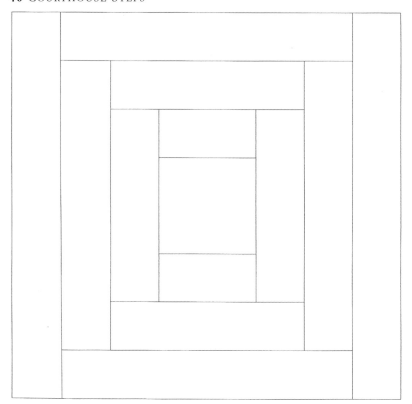

**Colourways**
Try placing colours on different sides of the block, altering the colour of the central square, using different shades of one colour for all the logs, or shading the logs from light to dark or the reverse.

**Quilt Settings**
As shown by the eight quilt settings overleaf, the blocks can be set in several different ways or used with traditional Log Cabin blocks to create a variety of designs.

**Block Pattern**
Use this 4in pattern as a guide to construct the block using foundation piecing, or hand or machine piecing, as described in Techniques. Start with the central square as for Traditional Log Cabin, but instead of building up the block by adding logs clockwise or anti-clockwise around the square, the logs are added to opposite sides alternately.

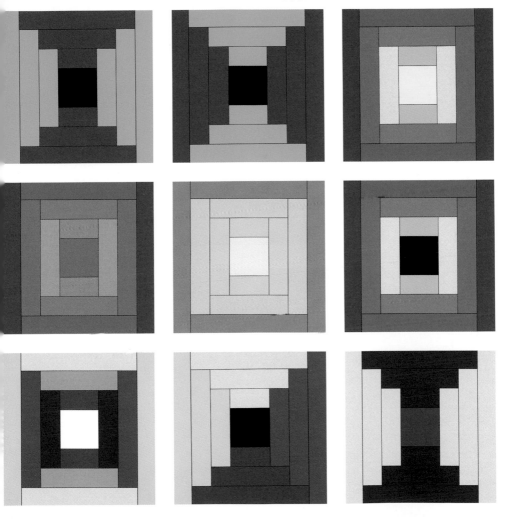

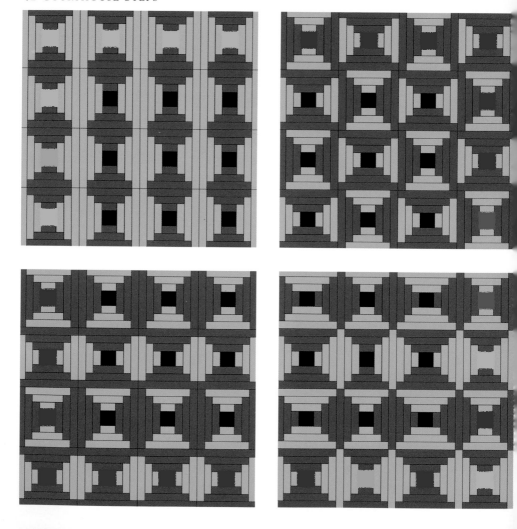

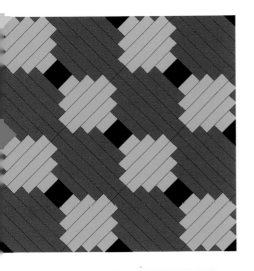

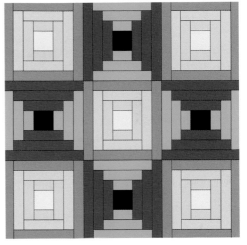

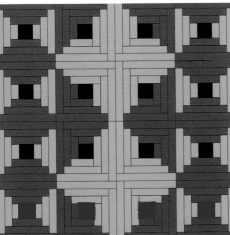

# PINEAPPLE

This Log Cabin variation is pieced around a central square on point (or diamond). A special Pineapple ruler will help in the construction of this more complicated variation and full details are provided with the ruler.

The block can also be pieced using folded triangles instead of the rhomboids and logs. If you examine the block carefully you will see that it is made up of a series of overlapping triangles. Set together, the horizontal and vertical shapes of the Pineapple Block create circles of colour across the quilt; make these the dominant colour in the quilt if you wish to emphasise this (see quilt settings, pages 48–9).

Moving the lighter colour to the diagonal blades emphasises the secondary circular pattern, while altering the shadings creates different secondary patterns where the blocks meet. You can also create the illusion of a medallion quilt – an intricate centre with one or more borders.

### Colourways

The nine colourways, right, show that placement of lights and darks can emphasise different parts, while the central square colour influences the perception of the log colours. Using white has a dramatic effect.

### Quilt Settings

Eight quilt settings are shown overleaf. As you can see, increasing the contrast between the two main colours further emphasises the pattern.

### Block Pattern

This pattern is for a 4in block. If you don't have a special Pineapple ruler then the easiest method of construction is foundation piecing.

If you choose to piece a block in a traditional manner, it will still need a foundation on which to mark the central horizontal, vertical and diagonal lines to ensure accuracy.

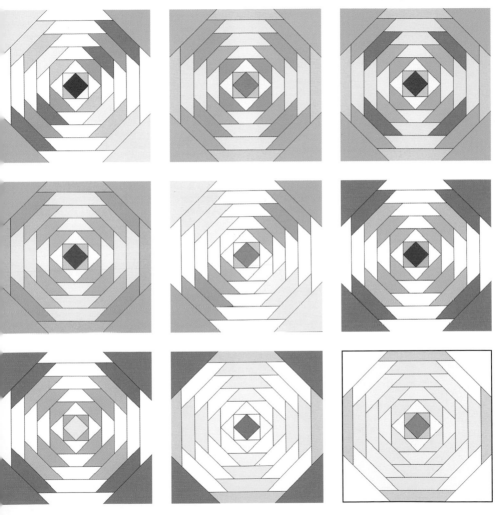

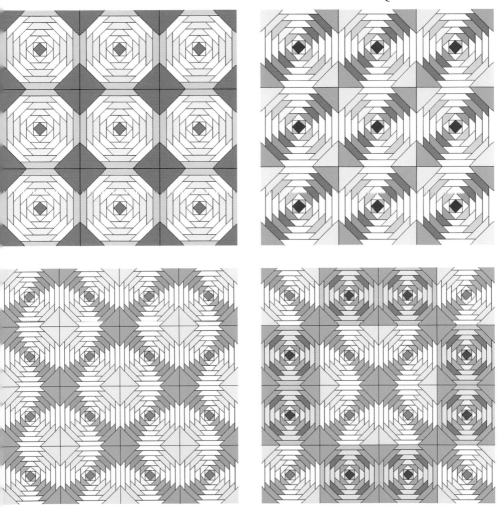

# HALF LOG CABIN

The full effect of this pattern can really only be appreciated when the finished blocks are made up into quilts.

This block can be set to produce the same types of design as the Traditional Log Cabin block when the block is shaded light and dark.

Interesting variations of the pattern can be produced by varying the width of the strips in each row or on each side (as in Quarter Log Cabin). Try splitting the logs – perhaps piecing each one from scraps – or adding a square or triangle to the corners to create new designs.

**Colourways**

Having the centre square and outer logs the same colour can produce some interesting patterns, whether straight set and rotated or set on point.

**Quilt Settings**

A great deal of variation can be achieved with this simple block, as shown by the eight quilt settings overleaf. Adding sashing between the blocks can produce a different effect.

**Block Pattern**

The 4in block shown here can be made using foundation piecing methods, traditional hand or machine piecing, or with folded logs (see Techniques). It is based on the Traditional Log Cabin block but is constructed around two sides of the square only.

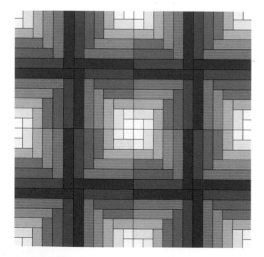
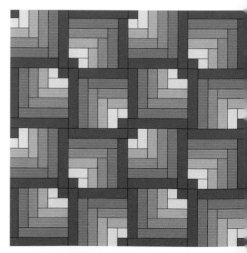

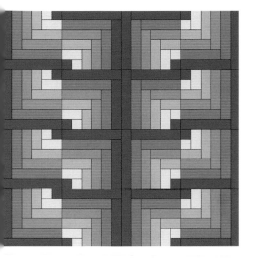

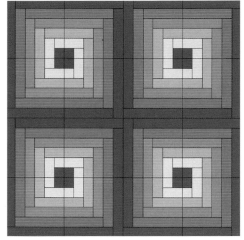

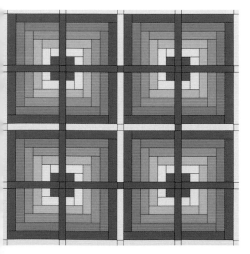

# OFF-CENTRE LOG CABIN

The off-centre look of this block is created by using logs of different widths. This quality gives the illusion of curves when the blocks are put together. The block is usually pieced with contrasting light and dark halves and by altering the placement of these shades you can alter the emphasis of the circles formed.

Try using different width logs in the same way around other shapes, around a rectangle for instance, or three different widths around a triangle, to create some exciting new designs. Exaggerating or minimising the difference in width between the logs can alter the circular effect; but too great a difference may result in a stepped appearance.

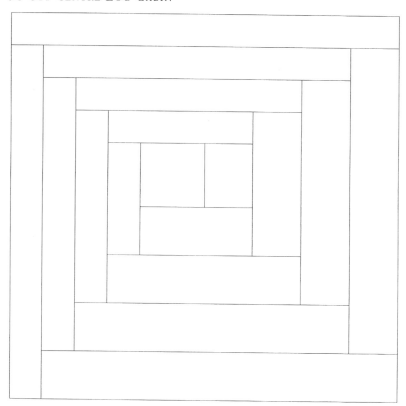

**Colourways**

The colourways shown opposite show the value of changing the colour of the centre square – it could be the same colour as one set of logs or a contrasting shade. You could also try shading the logs from light to dark.

**Quilt Settings**

The choice of colours substantially alters the look of a quilt, as can be seen by the stunningly different quilt settings overleaf.

**Block Pattern**

Use the 4in block given here as a guide to make templates or a foundation pattern. The block is constructed in exactly the same way as the Traditional Log Cabin block, following the instructions given in Techniques for your chosen method. Start with the central square and add logs around this square in the correct order until the block is complete.

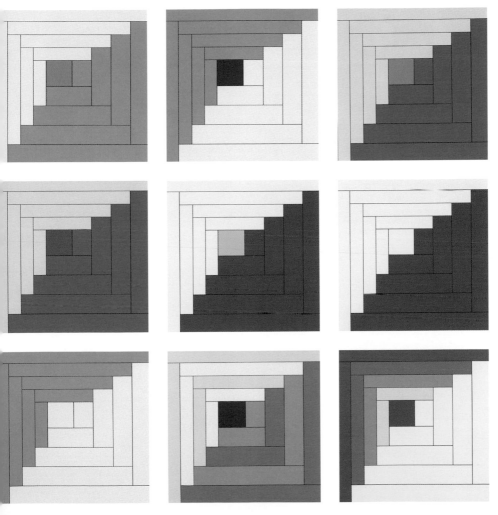

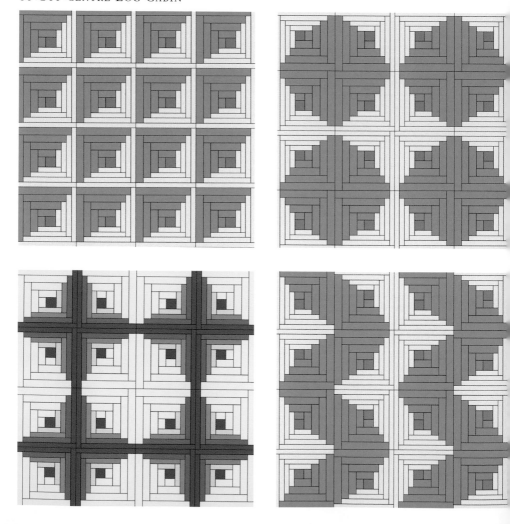

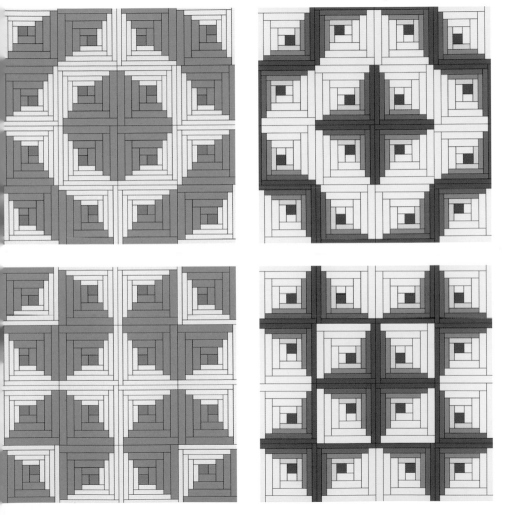

# RECTANGULAR LOG CABIN

This is a Log Cabin variation produced around a rectangle instead of a square and can be coloured in exactly the same way as traditional Log Cabin blocks. However, because the blocks are rectangular, a number of the traditional Log Cabin quilt designs cannot be made by simply turning the block through 90° as you would with a square block. A few examples of quilt settings are given on pages 66–7 to illustrate this.

The block pattern provided overleaf is 3in × 4½in but of course can be enlarged or reduced to any size you wish using graph paper or a photocopier, or the size can be converted to metric using metric graph paper.

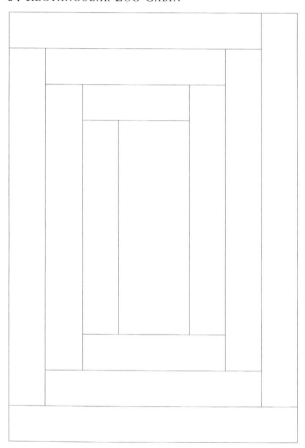

**Block Pattern**

The block is constructed in the same way as Traditional Log Cabin, starting with a central rectangle with logs sewn around until it is the right size, sewing an equal number of logs to both the long and short sides. If you want a square you will need to sew extra logs to the two long sides.

**Colourways**

Try changing the colour of the central rectangle or using shaded colours for the logs. Logs can be coloured in bands or spirals and the contrast between light and dark can be emphasised.

**Quilt Settings**

The first quilt setting overleaf shows a three-dimensional effect, producing an eyecatching pattern, most reminiscent of a well-known quilt pattern called Attic Windows. Note also the effect of introducing a contrast colour within the block.

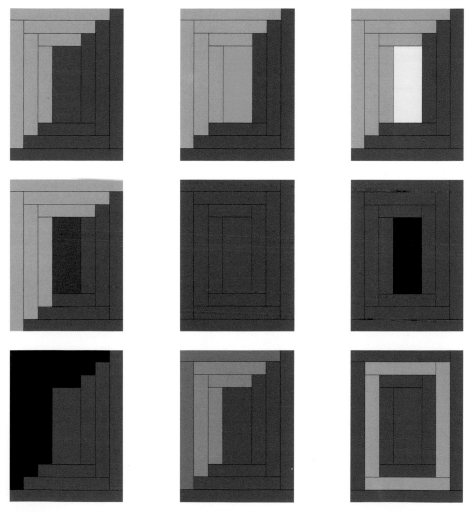

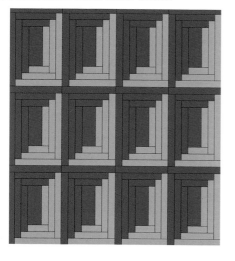

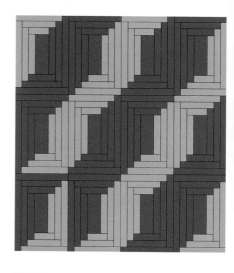

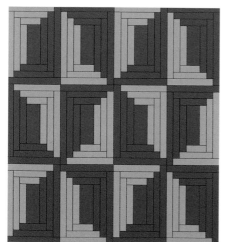

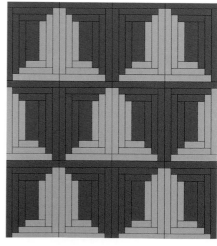

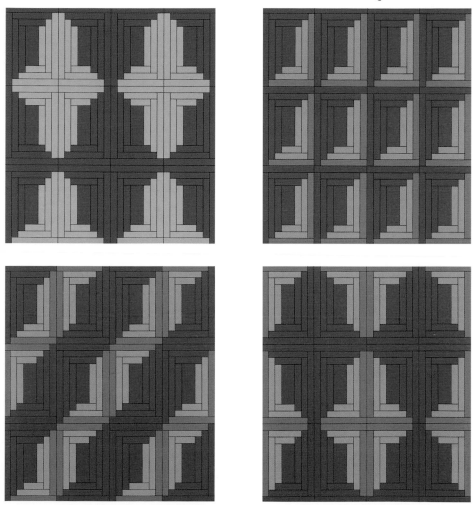

# MARCHING TRIANGLES

This variation of Courthouse Steps has a central square divided diagonally and triangles added to one end of one set of logs. The colour placement of the logs is usually light and dark opposite each other with the triangles in a strongly contrasting colour.

Marching Triangle blocks can be set in a number of ways. They can be coloured and set as traditional Log Cabin style blocks or a combination of Log Cabin and Courthouse Steps can be used. The addition of contrasting triangles to the traditional Log Cabin or Courthouse Steps designs creates an interesting range of secondary patterns when blocks are put together.

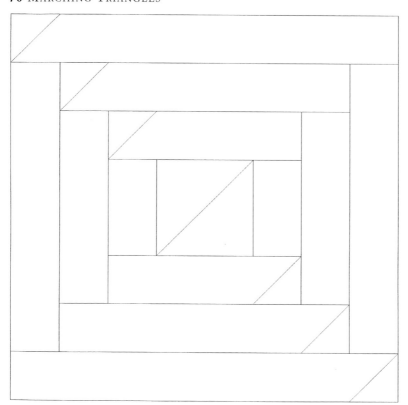

## Colourways

Try colouring the logs the same way as traditional Log Cabin – half light, half dark; or shade the logs or triangles across either the block or the quilt, or change the colours of the central triangles.

## Quilt Settings

The quilt settings overleaf show that the triangles give an added dimension to this design. Sashing and setting the blocks on point also changes the look of the overall pattern.

## Block Pattern

As a Courthouse Steps variation this can be pieced in the same way. Start by piecing the central square, then add the short logs to either side for the first round. Add the triangles to the next pair of logs before sewing them to the central square. The triangles can be folded to provide an added dimension.

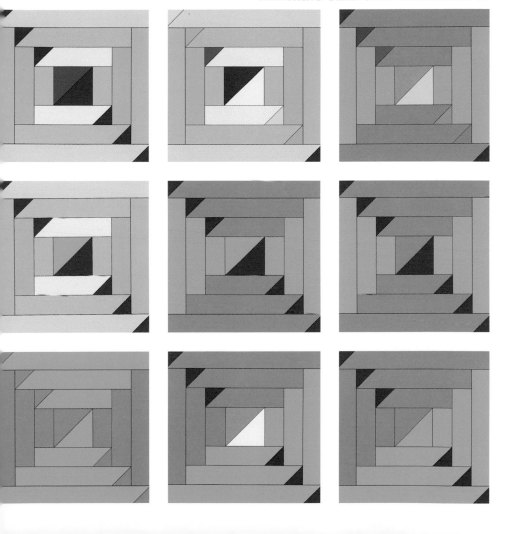

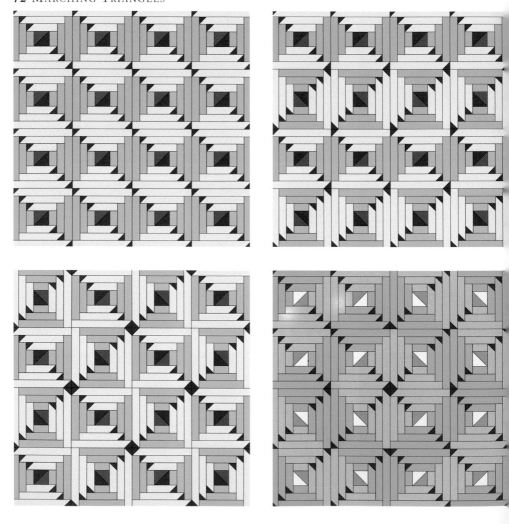

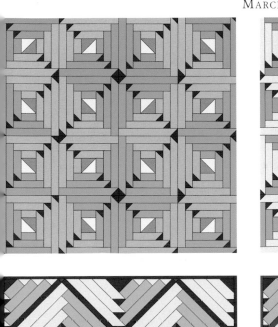

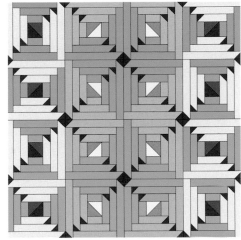

# WILD GOOSE

This variation can be constructed using traditional hand or machine piecing, or foundation piecing with folded triangles (see Techniques). The colouring of the block is a variation of Courthouse Steps, with greater contrast provided by the triangles.

The triangles in this block are reminiscent of the Flying Geese pattern often found in strip quilts or borders and its name probably reflects this. As with Marching Triangles, the addition of triangles to the block creates the opportunity for a range of secondary patterns to be formed; changing as the shading or colouring of the triangles is altered.

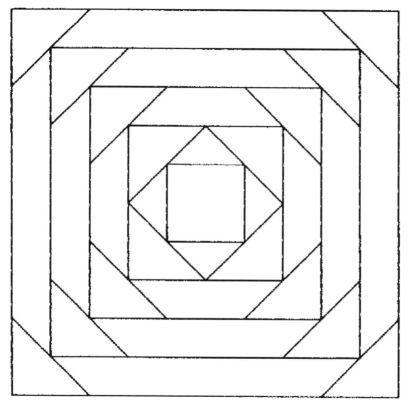

**Colourways**
The colours of the logs, or triangles, can be shaded light to dark – this shading could be carried out across the quilt; or the triangles could be two colours.

**Quilt Settings**
These blocks can be set like Courthouse Steps. Notice the difference that sashing – and its colour – can make to the appearance of a quilt.

**Block Pattern**
Use the 4in pattern given to make templates or to act as a guide. The block can be constructed using traditional methods, or quick piecing, to piece the individual logs first before piecing the block as a whole. It is not really suitable for foundation piecing unless you use folded triangles.

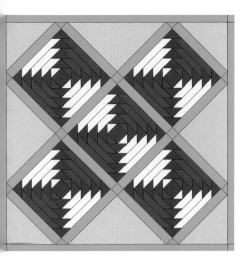

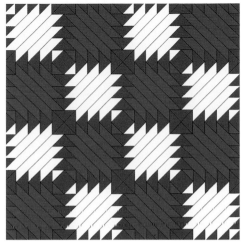

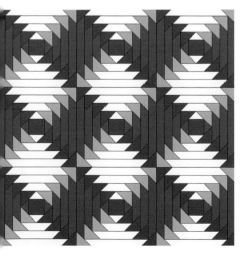

# STEPPING STONES

T his variation is so-called because of the stepped pattern created by the small squares added at the junction of each round of logs radiating from the larger central square.

The block can be coloured as either Log Cabin or Courthouse Steps. Ideally the central square and the smaller squares should all be the same colour and contrast with the other colour(s) used in the block but the colourways shown overleaf suggest other combinations.

This block gives an example of pieced logs. Try piecing logs in other ways – by adding squares in the centre instead of the corner perhaps. Another variation – Chimney Corners – has squares just at the outermost corners of the block.

**Colourways**
Try using differen[t] shades of the sam[e] colour or two different colours, each running in opposite direction[s] colouring the centre square to give a blended, transparent effect[.]

**Quilt Settings**
The quilt settings overleaf show a few examples of the different methods of colouring the block and show the effect of adding sashing.

**Block Pattern**
This block should be pieced using traditional hand or machine piecing. The construction is similar to that for Courthouse Steps. Starting with the centre square, sew the first pair of logs to either side, then sew a pieced pair of logs – with small squares at both ends – to the other two sides. Continue until the block is complete.

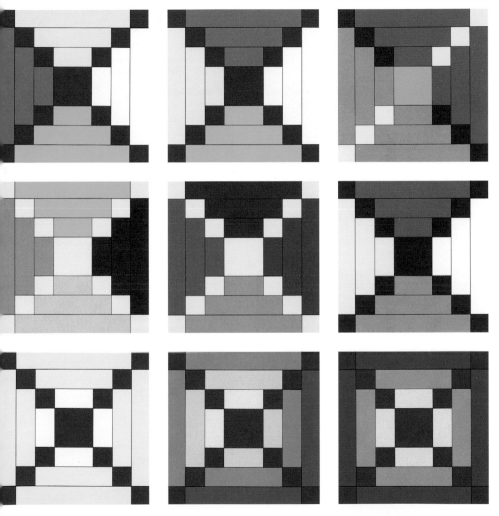

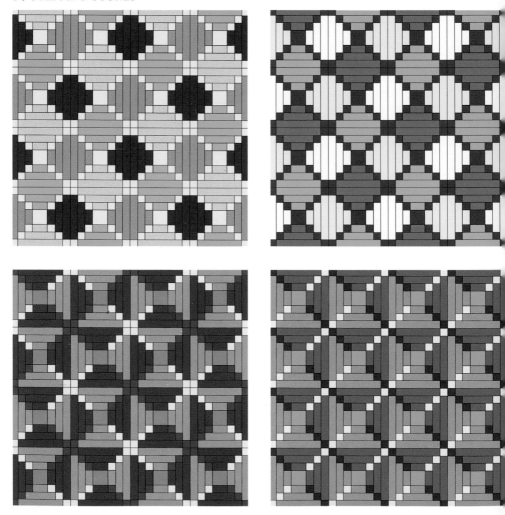

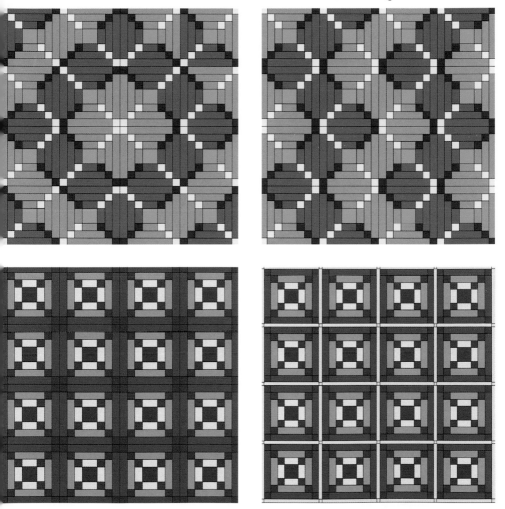

# SPLIT-CENTRE LOG CABIN

A s its name implies, this variation of Log Cabin has the central square subdivided into two rectangles. This can emphasise the colour split between the two halves of the block or be used as a complete contrast.

This block is an easy introduction to the idea of splitting or piecing the central square. You could perhaps try increasing the size of the centre square (reducing the number of logs if necessary) and piecing a miniature block instead of a plain square. Some examples are shown in Further Log Cabin Variations on page 122. A motif cut from a novelty fabric can also be used to good effect as a central square, as shown in the quilted Christmas wall hanging on page 9.

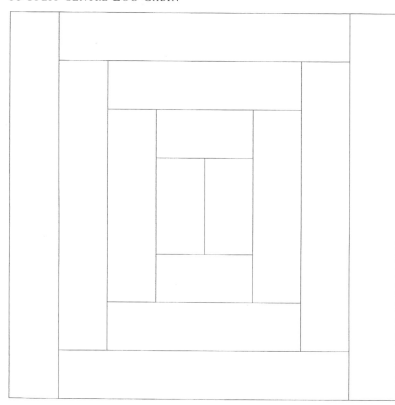

## Colourways
The block is usually coloured in the same way as Log Cabin or Courthouse Steps.

## Quilt Settings
Both Courthouse Steps and Log Cabin colourings have been used to illustrate these quilt settings. Notice the difference that changing the colours or the colour placement of the two central rectangles makes. You can also change the emphasis of light and dark shades, or shade the logs from light to dark within their colour ranges.

## Block Pattern
Use this 4in pattern as a guide to construct the block in exactly the same way as the Courthouse Steps block – once the centre square has been pieced by joining the two rectangles, follow your chosen construction method.

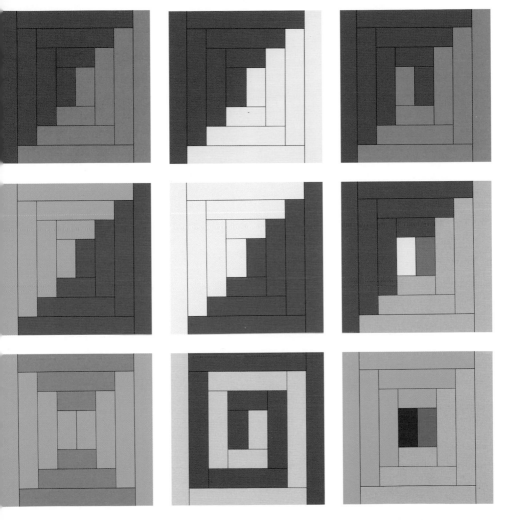

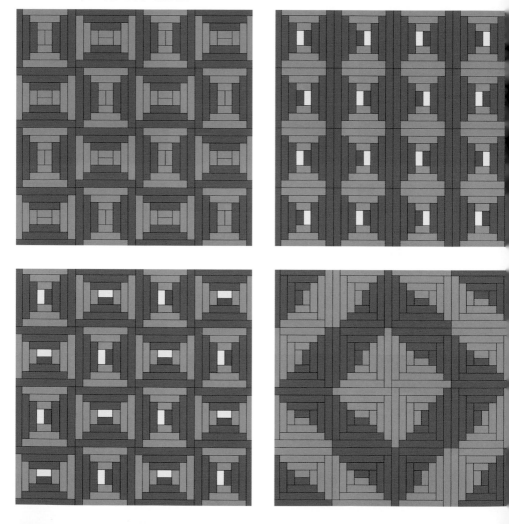

# QUARTER LOG CABIN

This Log Cabin variation is similar to Half Log Cabin but is pieced around a corner rectangle instead of a square and has different width logs in the two halves of the square. It can pieced as a rectangular block by having the same width strips on both sides of the rectangle.

Although using different width strips in the two halves of this block, the design does not produce the curves seen in Off-centre Log Cabin. Instead, when blocks are put together, larger bands of colour can be formed, particularly where the wider logs meet, and shading these creates some interest. Lightning streaks can be made to zigzag down the quilt, or pinwheels can appear.

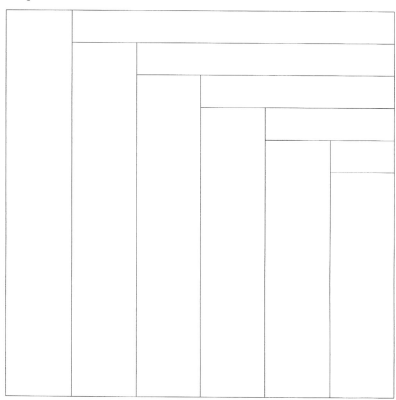

**Colourways**

The block is coloured in two contrasting colours for the narrow and wide strips and the colours can be shaded light to dark. Shading the colours of the block gives a three-dimensional effect when they are put together.

**Quilt Settings**

Bands of colour can be introduced – the full effect of these seen only when four blocks are put together. Adding sashing either to shaded blocks or to banded blocks creates other patterns.

**Block Pattern**

This block can be pieced using foundation piecing, traditional or folded methods. Start with the corner rectangle and add the first narrow log followed by the first wide log. Continue adding logs in this fashion – narrow then wide – to the two sides of the corner rectangle until the block is complete.

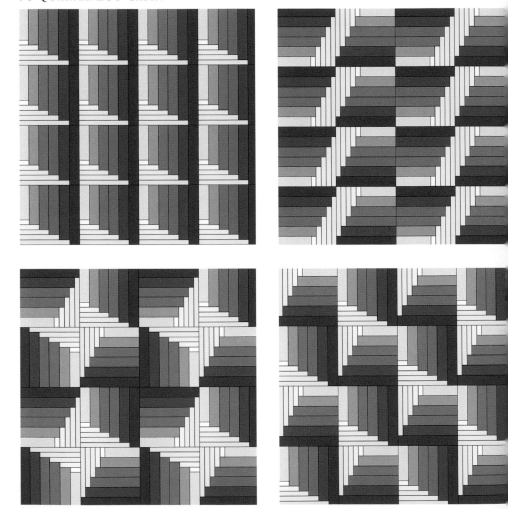

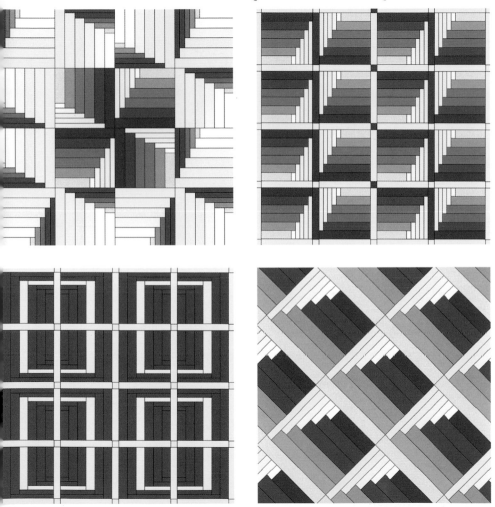

# DIAMOND IN THE SQUARE

This block is a Courthouse Steps variation and is pieced in a similar way to Wild Goose. The triangles should form a strong contrast to the other two colours used in the block. These, together with the logs, can be shaded from light to dark either across the block or across the quilt.

This block shows another example of a pieced central square. The triangles, as in Wild Goose and Marching Triangles, form interesting secondary patterns in addition to those formed by the Log Cabin, especially if the colour or shading of the triangles is altered. Careful shading of the logs could give the effect of a ribbon wound around the central square.

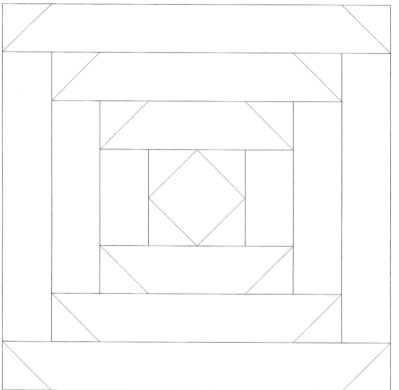

## Colourways
The colour placement for the logs can follow that of Courthouse Steps or Traditional Log Cabin. Alternatively, bands of colour can be introduced.

## Quilt Settings
Using several different, but related, block colourways in the quilt can add interest and increase the number of possible designs.

## Block Pattern
Use the 4in pattern as a guide to construct this block using any of the methods described in Techniques. Start with the central diamond and add the triangles to make the central square. The first two logs are then added. The triangles can be pieced or folded and are added as the logs are sewn.

# LOG CABIN RIBBONS

This variation is based on Half Log Cabin with split logs and flying geese triangles added at the junction of the logs. The block can be coloured in a multitude of different ways, though the triangles should provide quite a strong contrast to the rest of the block.

Most of the Log Cabin designs lend themselves to this treatment – the logs are pieced, then subdivided into a series of squares, rectangles or triangles to form patterns across a quilt. Interesting woven effects can be achieved or, as with this design, a series of very different secondary patterns can be created. Experiment with some of the blocks to see a variety of possibilities.

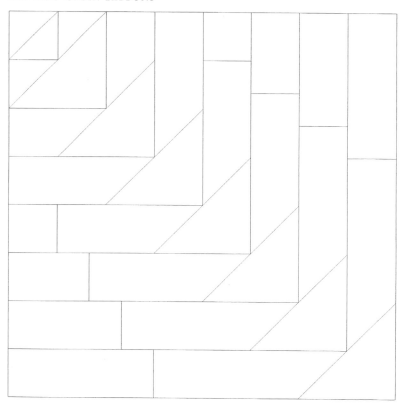

## Colourways

The pieced logs can be darker than the others, and the added triangles a very strong contrast to the rest of the block, emphasising the secondary patterns when the blocks are joined.

## Quilt Settings

Notice how altering the placement of colours in the logs and triangles can affect the look of the quilt. Using two mirror-image colourways in one quilt is very effective. Changing the rotation of the blocks produces different patterns where the blocks meet when joined.

## Block Pattern

Traditional piecing is probably the easiest option for this block. Piece the individual logs first, adding the triangles at the end of each round.

These triangles can be folded and inserted during piecing to add a further dimension to the quilt; in this case make the logs from complete rectangles, not rhomboids.

# RITA'S WHIRLIES

This block has been pioneered by internationally known UK quiltmaker and teacher, Rita Humphry – hence its name. It is pieced around a central square on point in the same way as a traditional Log Cabin design is constructed and can therefore be considered as a variation of this block. This block can also be pieced around other shapes such as triangles and hexagons.

Rita Humphry suggests that the central square should be very dark, that two opposite bands should be light/neutral, and that the other two opposite bands should be dark shading to light. Other suggestions are made in colourways overleaf.

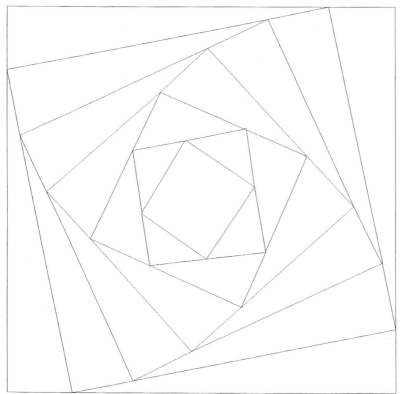

## Colourways
Some colour suggestions are illustrated, including a light central square; contrasting colours in the bands; and the central square the same colour as one set of bands.

## Quilt Settings
This block is so versatile – look at the number of patterns that emerge from one simple colouring just by different rotations of the blocks. The last quilt shows the blocks on point with setting triangles to match the centre squares.

## Block Pattern
It is best to foundation piece this block as it is easier to keep it symmetrical and the pieces in the right place. Start with the central square and add pieces around this in a clockwise direction until the block is finished. Complete details on how to draft and construct the block are given in the *Quilt Room Patchwork and Quilting Workshops* (see Bibliography).

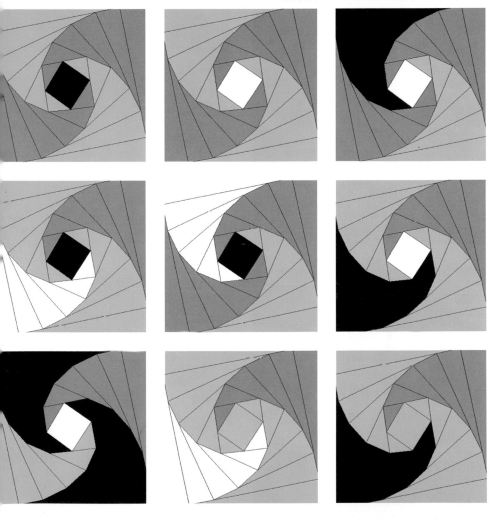

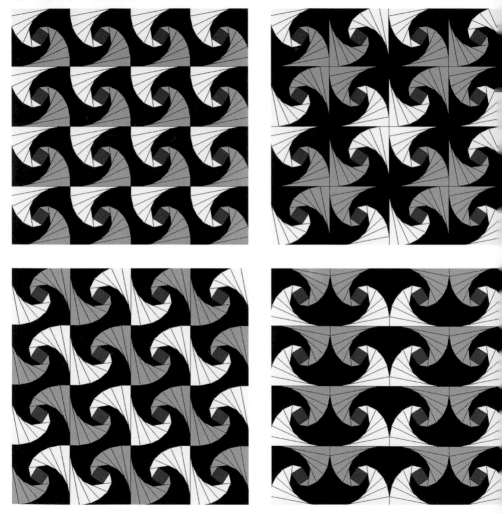

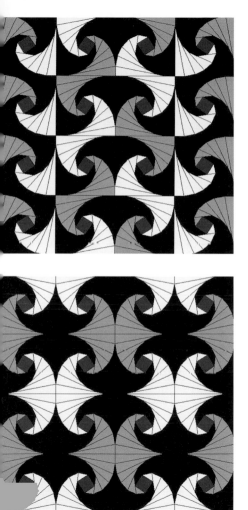

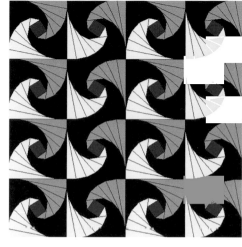

# CRAZY LOG CABIN

As the name implies, there is no set pattern for this block, though it resembles a traditional Log Cabin design in that there is a central shape and that pieces are added around it in the same way.

Crazy Log Cabins can be fairly ordered by using the same arrangement of colours and pieces in each block, or very random by ensuring that each block is different either in the placement of colours or the shapes of the pieces. There is no rule which states that quilt blocks must be square, just make sure that you can join all the blocks together at the end!

**Colourways**

As with all the Log Cabin variations you can alter the colour of the central square or the shading and contrast between the colours in the block.

**Quilt Settings**

As this is a crazy block, why not add an unexpected colour in one tiny patch – a contrast colour in one of the corners will create a secondary pattern, as shown in the quilt settings overleaf.

**Block Pattern**

You can alter this pattern to create your own foundation pieced crazy designs. Start with the central shape and gradually build up the block, adding pieces around the central square in turn. If a piece is too small when it is flipped back there is no need to remove it, just cut the next piece larger so that it covers the gap.

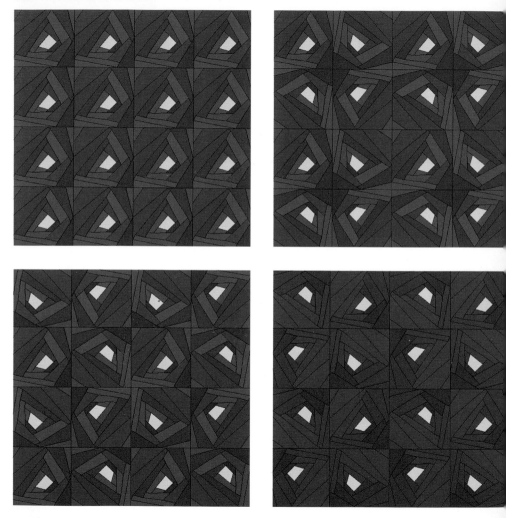

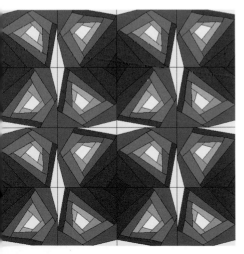

# FURTHER VARIATIONS

A multitude of other variations on the Log Cabin are possible, encompassing many different colourways, shapes and patterns. A few of them are shown here, but part of the fun of this block is in designing your own variations.

The logs and the central square can be subdivided, the logs can be drawn different widths, and, of course, the technique can be used to sew strips around other geometric shapes.

**House**

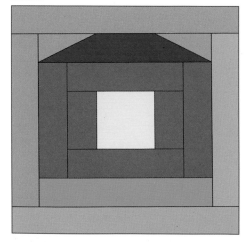

**Sailing Boat**

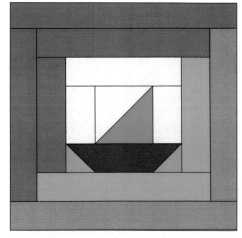

**Hidden Star**

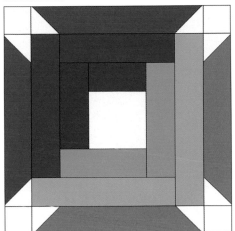

**Variation of Half Log Cabin**

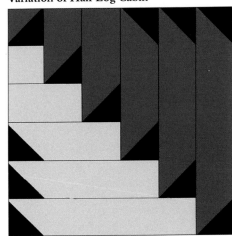

**Star in the Centre**

**Narrow and Wide Variation**

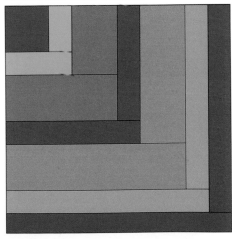

**Dutchman's Puzzle**

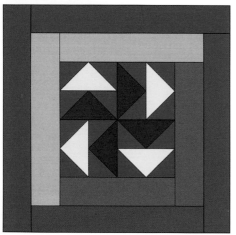

**Hexagon**

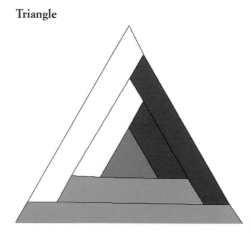

**Diamond Log Cabin**

**Triangle**

**Octagon**

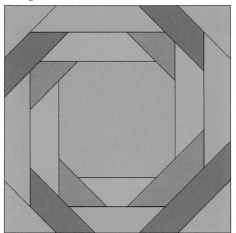

**Interlaced Cabin**

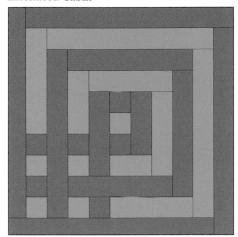

**Log Cabin with Folded Triangle Corners**

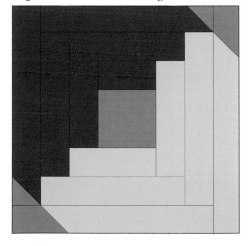

**Woven Cabin**

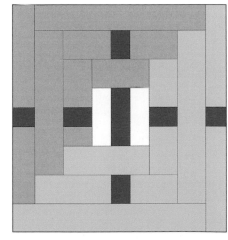

**Greek Key**

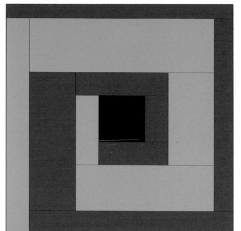

**Squares in the Corners**

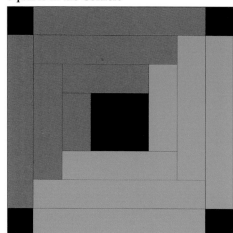

**Pinwheels**

**Half Log Cabin with Triangles**

# BIBLIOGRAPHY

This is not intended as a comprehensive list of quilting books, just some that you may find useful.

Campbell Harding, Valerie, *Strip Patchwork* (Batsford, 1989)

Causee, Linda, *101 Log Cabin Blocks* (American School of Needlework, 1997)

Chainey, Barbara, *The Essential Quilter* (David & Charles, 1993)

Cox, Patricia, *The Log Cabin Workbook* (One of a Kind Quilting Designs, 1980, 2nd edition)

Denton, Susan and Macey, Barbara, *Quiltmaking* (David & Charles, 1987)

Fanning, Robbie and Fanning, Tony, *The Complete Book of Machine Quilting* (Chilton, 1980)

Gadd, Kerry, *Beyond Log Cabin* (That Patchwork Place, 1999)

Hargreave, Harriet, *Heirloom Machine Quilting* (C&T Publishing, 1990)

Hopkins, Mary Ellen, *A Log Cabin Notebook* (ME Publications, 1991)

Lintott, Pam and Miller, Rosemary (compilers), *The Quilt Room Patchwork and Quilting Workshops* (Letts, 1992)

Martin, Judy, *Scraps, Blocks and Quilts* (Crossley-Griffith, 1990)

McCalls Easy Big Blocks – Tissue paper foundation patterns: B501 Log Cabin, B509 Pineapple, B521 Diamond Log Cabin

McDonald, Deidre, *Quilt Treasures* (The Quilter's Guild, 1995)

Mitchell, Marti, *Creating Curves with Log Cabin* (American School of Needlework, 1997)

Mitchell, Marti, *Weekend Log Cabin Quilts* (American School of Needlework, 1991)

Rae, Janet, *The Quilts of the British Isles* (McDonald Books, 1996, new edition)

Seward, Linda, *Patchwork, Appliqué and Quilting* (Mitchell Beazley, 1996, revised edition)

Wein, Carol Anne, *The Log Cabin Quilt Book* (Westbridge Books, 1985)

Wood, Kay, *Starmakers Ablaze Vol. I – Log Cabin Triangles* (EZ International, 1988)

Wood, Kay, *Starmakers Ablaze Vol. II – Log Cabin Diamonds* (EZ International, 1987)

# INDEX

# ACKNOWLEDGEMENTS

With many thanks to Barbara, who started it all. To Arnot and Rebecca (who helped design the quilts) for putting up with the more than usual haphazard domestic engineering, and for sorting out problems with the computer. To Liane Purnell for making many of the blocks. To Patricia Cox for allowing access to and photographs of her wonderful collection of quilts; and to members of the Quilters' Guild of the British Isles and Staffordshire Patchworkers for their friendship, help and advice. The blocks and quilts were drawn with the aid of the Electric Quilt computer program EQ4, supplied by Rio Designs; thanks also to Lawrence Dawes of Rio for his help.